The Parisian Café:
A Literary
Companion

Selected & Edited
by Val Clark

UNIVERSE

A fontaste of
Paris to prepare
your visit in
September ...
See you soon !

Clémence

First published in the United States of America in 2002 by

UNIVERSE PUBLISHING
A Division of Rizzoli International Publications, Inc.
300 Park Avenue South
New York, NY 10010

2002 2003 2004 2005 2006 2007/ 10 9 8 7 6 5 4 3 2 1

Printed in Hong Kong
ISBN: 0-7893-0673-5

Library of Congress Control Number: 2002108483

Front Cover: LOVERS IN A CAFE, ca. 1932
Brassaï

Back Cover: THE WAY A POEM OF ADY'S BEGAN ON A CAFE TABLE IN PARIS, ca. 1928
André Kertész

To my mom and dad, who inspired in me a love of the arts.

I would like to thank my publisher, Charles Miers, my editor, Jessica Fuller, and the book's designer, Amelia Costigan, for sharing my enthusiasm for Parisian cafés and bringing this book to life.

In addition, special thanks go to my brother, Brad, who took me to all the Parisian cafés, and Mary Ellen Russell, whose steadfast support encouraged me to complete this project.

Finally, my sincere thanks go to all the writers and artists represented in these pages, as well as to their publishers, agents, and representatives.

The Parisian café has long been a haven for artists and writers.

Throughout history it has played an essential role in some of the world's greatest literary and artistic achievements, collaborations, and friendships. For over 300 years, tree-lined boulevards, gilded, mirrored walls, and marble-topped tables have stood witness to and have come to define a golden era of the café. Cafés came into existence as early as 1686, when Café Procope became the first place of its kind in Paris to serve coffee indoors.

By 1843 there were over 3,000 cafés in the City of Light. In his *Histoire de France,* Jules Michelet places the emergence of the café at the forefront of his country's cultural development:

> *Paris becomes one great coffeehouse. . . . Never did Paris talk more or better. . . . Wit sprang forth, spontaneous, where it might and as it could.*

Artists and writers of every kind flourished at the café. For the Impressionists, it was an essential meeting place. During 1866–1869, Edouard Manet, Edgar Degas, Camille Pissarro, Auguste Renoir, and Claude Monet met regularly at the Café Guerbois. Before these artists were ever known as "Impressionists," they were referred to as the "Batignolles Group," because they frequented a café on the rue des Batignolles. Like photographers decades later, the Impressionists incorporated café life into their art. Edouard Manet made the café, its waiters, and its patrons a central theme in some of his greatest paintings, such as *Woman Reading in a Café,* 1879.

Throughout the centuries, artists and writers have found creative inspiration at the café. Whether a small café on a little winding side street or a grand café in the heart of the city, the stage was set. It was here that they found one another; here that they shared good times and bad; here that they flourished. As one becomes better acquainted with their lives, common traits emerge: they all shared a passion for the arts, a thirst for life, and a need for the café.

Anaïs Nin once wrote, "The hours I have spent in cafés are the only ones I call living, apart from writing." When she met Henry Miller in 1931, their legendary relationship began and would span a lifetime. The café was an essential element in this relationship; Miller was notorious for making optimal use of café stationery, and many of his letters addressed to her are from cafés all over Paris; to see them transports one back to those glorious café days. He wrote to Anaïs on February 7, 1932, that

> *Proust is going to my head. . . . This afternoon I was reading him in the Café Mirroir. . . . From time to time I looked up and allowed my eyes to rest on the string of café crèmes that ran from one end of the hall to the other.*

In the same month and year, Anaïs remarks in her diary:

> *Henry's letters give me a feeling of plenitude I get rarely. They are extraordinary. I take great joy in answering them.*

Jean-Paul Sartre and Simone de Beauvoir were another inseparable pair whose lives and writing became intertwined with café life. Theirs was a famous café romance. They met, worked, and practically lived at the Café de Flore. When friends, students, or colleagues wished to find them, they knew to stop by the Flore. In fact, the café eventually received so many calls for them that the owner gave them a private phone. During the wartime years when they often could not be together, they wrote to one another from—and always made reference to—their favorite café; in January 1941, Simone de Beauvoir wrote to Sartre:

> *I'm upstairs at the Flore and it's seven in the evening. It's agreeable, because you can hear all*

*the people swarming beneath you, yet you're
totally peaceful. . . . I've regained all my peace
of mind, since I had news of you and began
writing to you again.*

And in the summer of 1943, Sartre wrote to de
Beauvoir:

*How far away you are. I miss you . . . Paris is
so dull when you aren't here to see what I'm seeing
at the same time I see it. . . . It's five o'clock, it's
Saturday, I'm upstairs at the Flore, the sun is
coming in the window.*

The Parisian café became a place of solace and
refuge to other artists and writers in different ways.
When they were apart and things were not going well
between them, Zelda Fitzgerald wrote to her husband,
F. Scott Fitzgerald, in 1931 from a clinic in Switzerland:

*Was it fun . . . did the blue creep out from
behind the Colonades of the rue de Rivoli through
the grill of the Tuileries . . . and did the trees
hang brooding over the cafés and were there*

*lights at night and the click of saucers and the
auto horns that play de Bussey (sic).*

In turn, Fitzgerald sets his short story "Babylon
Revisited" along the same boulevards; at one point his
narrator almost paraphrases Zelda's letter:

*He wanted to see the blue hour spread over the
magnificent facade, and imagine . . . the cab
horns, playing endlessly the first few bars of* Les
Plus que Lent.

It was also in the Parisian café where some of America's most promising young African-American poets, writers, and performers— such as Langston Hughes, Richard Wright, James Baldwin, and Josephine Baker—experienced an exhilarating new freedom, where color was not an issue. In fact, these artists came into their own here and even took Paris by storm.

Even for those who were down-trodden or disillusioned, setting foot inside the café became an instinctual act of hope. When Modigliani was starving and penniless, he could be found at the Rotonde, sketching portraits of café patrons, earning enough in a few hours to get him through the day. When Giacometti became discouraged after working all day in his studio, he could be found at a back table inside the Dome, sculpting his magically intricate miniature sculptures.

For the great photographers, the café became a central focus. Eugene Atget documented the historical

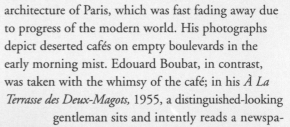

architecture of Paris, which was fast fading away due to progress of the modern world. His photographs depict deserted cafés on empty boulevards in the early morning mist. Edouard Boubat, in contrast, was taken with the whimsy of the café; in his *À La Terrasse des Deux-Magots,* 1955, a distinguished-looking gentleman sits and intently reads a newspaper with the aid of a monocle. A sophisticated poodle sits attentively beside him at a separate table and seems to stare knowingly at the photographer. Robert Doisneau also celebrated the café's patrons; he captured such café regulars as Simone de Beauvoir, Jean-Paul Sartre, Jacques Prevert, Alberto Giacometti, and others at work or play in their favorite café. André Kertész also focused on writers and artists at the cafés, but emphasized more their relationships with one another. With a sensitive eye and a poet's soul, he sought dreamier, more ephemeral moments, and hence captured the café's warmth and intimacy. One example is a self-portrait depicting him with his childhood sweetheart entitled *Elizabeth and Me in a Montparnasse Café*, 1931.

Brassaï's photographic style is starker, more sensual, and evocative of Paris café life. He is perhaps best remembered for his works depicting Paris café life after-hours, such as *Lovers in a Café*, 1932. The lure of these eerily deserted nocturnal scenes and the rich contrast of the electrically lit cafés against the pitch darkness of night inspired Henry Miller to name Brassaï, "The Eye of Paris."

For Ernest Hemingway, the cafés of Paris were indispensable; he wrote not only in them but also about them, more so, arguably, than any other author. Cafés appear time and again in some of his greatest short stories—such as "A Clean, Well-Lighted Place"—and also serve as a central setting in his early novel *The Sun Also Rises*. Decades later, in *A Moveable Feast*, he recalls:

> *I came to a good café that I knew on the Place St.-Michel. It was a pleasant café, warm and clean and friendly, and I hung up my old waterproof on the coat rack to dry and put my worn and weathered felt hat on the rack above the bench and ordered a café au lait. The waiter brought it and I took out a notebook from the pocket of the coat and a pencil and started to write.*

Today, the café remains a place where the awnings, tables, and chairs await you; a place where you may arrive feeling blue, and then, for no apparent reason, find the mood magically lifting; maybe an idea comes to mind, a friend approaches, the coffee is served. Or perhaps the sun comes out, a breeze stirs, or a favorite song is played. But one thing is evident: at the café one realizes one is not so alone as previously supposed and that life itself can be grand. As Jean-Paul Sartre once noted in *Being and Nothingness*:

> *It is certain that the café by itself with its patrons, its tables, its booths, its mirrors, its light, its smoky atmosphere, and the sounds of voices, rattling saucers, and footsteps which fill it—the café is a fullness of being.*

You start at a café table because every-

thing in Paris starts at a café table.

—Irwin Shaw, *Paris! Paris!*

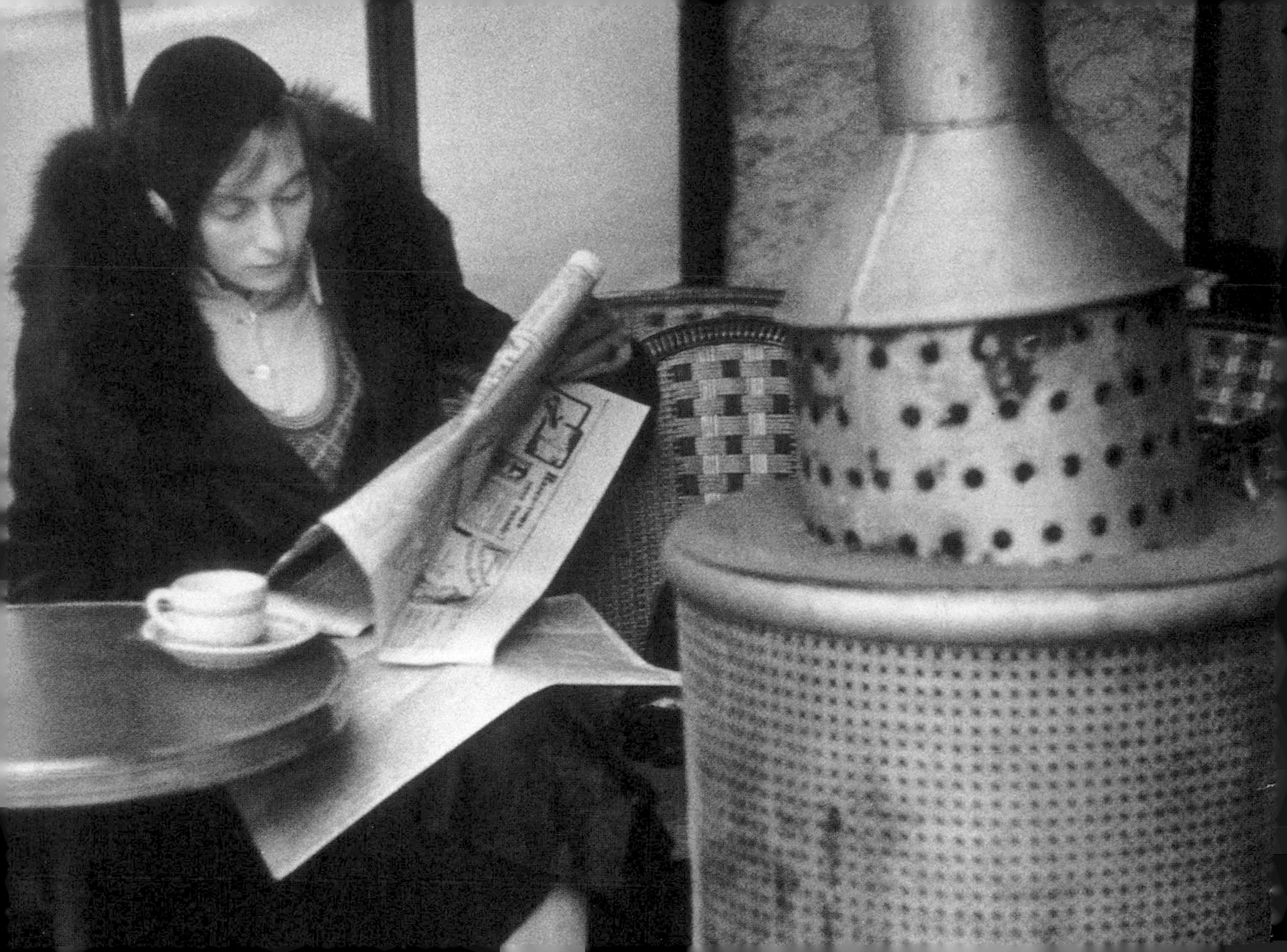

CAFÉ LE DOME, 1931
Seeberger Brothers

The little cafés at five in the morning—their

windows steamed over—boiling hot coffee.

—Albert Camus, *Notebooks 1935–1942*

Does black coffee make you drunk, do you think? I felt quite *envirée* . . . and could have sat three years, smoking and sipping and thinking and watching the flakes of snow. And then you know the strange silence that falls upon your heart—the same silence that comes one minute before the curtain rises. I felt that and knew that I should write here.

—Katherine Mansfield, in a letter to John Middleton Murry, March 19, 1915

Jean Béraud

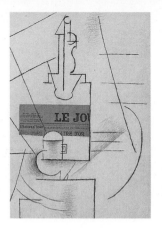

BOTTLE, CUP AND NEWSPAPER,
Paris, autumn–winter 1912
Pablo Picasso

Right: PICASSO INSIDE THE CAFÉ
FLORE, 1939
Brassaï

In their lettered canvases, both men [Picasso and Braque] repeatedly used *Le Journal*, their favorite newspaper—pictorially, anyhow. At first they inserted its name in full, and then in abbreviations, such as JOURN, JOUR, JOU or even LEJO, all of which made it the Paris daily with the most artistic unpaid publicity in newspaper history.

—Janet Flanner, *Men & Monuments: Profiles of Picasso, Matisse, Braque, & Malraux*

Without cafés and newspapers, it would be difficult to travel. A paper printed in our own language, a place to rub shoulders with others in the evenings enable us to imitate the familiar gestures of the man we were at home, who, seen from a distance, seems so much a stranger.

—Albert Camus, *Love of Life*

GIACOMETTI IN A CAFÉ, 1958
Robert Doisneau

Giacometti had just gotten up. He was on his way to the café to have some coffee and I went with him. The café has come to be something of an adjunct to his studio.

—James Lord, *A Giacometti Portrait*

HEMINGWAY (FAR LEFT) AND
FRIENDS ON A CAFÉ TERRACE, 1925
Anonymous

Following page left: JEAN-PAUL SARTRE,
CAFÉ DE FLORE, 1945
Brassaï

Following page right: SIMONE DE BEAUVOIR
IN THE CAFÉ DES DEUX-MAGOTS, 1945
Robert Doisneau

I had the feeling that this [Paris] was the best place in the world for an artist to live

and work. . . . The prevalence of the sidewalk café was an important factor. It gave

easy access to one's friends and gave extra pleasure to long walks through various parts

of the city. . . . There was a seeming timelessness about the place that was conducive to

the kind of contemplation essential to art.

—Stuart Davis, *Autobiography*

À SAINT-GERMAIN-DES-PRÈS, 1959
Sergio Larrain

DEUX-MAGOTS from *Madeline's Rescue*
Ludwig Bemelmans

Right: CAFÉ DES DEUX-MAGOTS
Ludwig Bemelmans

It is the wide piece of sidewalk whereon stand the red marble-topped tables, the wicker chairs, and the old waiters of the Café des Deux Magots. From it you can look undisturbed at the chalk-colored walls and the tower of the church of St.-Germain-des-Pres. . . . Nuns with white butterfly hats come out of the church. . . .

This corner I love best of all in Paris, and here I sat down in peace.

—Ludwig Bemelmans, *My English Suit in Paris*

Paris as seen by the morning sun of three or four and twenty and Paris in the twilight of the superfluous decade cannot be expected to look exactly alike. I well remember my first breakfast at a Parisian café in the spring of 1833. It was in the Place de la Bourse, on a beautiful sunshiny morning. The coffee was nectar, the *flute* was ambrosia, the *brioche* was more than good enough for the Olympians. Such an experience could not repeat itself fifty years later.

—Oliver Wendell Holmes, *Our Hundred Days in Europe*

Right: PARIS, JULY 1952
Robert Capa

AT THE CAFÉ FLORE IN MONTPARNASSE, ca. 1950s
Sanford Roth

There is in London perhaps one waiter to every five thousand persons;
whereas in Paris there are five thousand waiters, more or less, to every one
person. Or so it seems. It is a city of waiters; it is *the* city of waiters.

—E. V. Lucas, *A Wanderer in Paris*

rendez-vous du monde entier

the meeting place of all the world

Le Café de la Paix

P aintings and music, street noises, shops, flower markets, modes, fabrics,

poems, ideas, everything seemed to lead toward a half-sensual, half-intellectual

swoon. Inside the cafés, color, perfume, taste and delirium could be poured together

from one bottle or many bottles —from square, cylindrical, conical, tall, squat, brown,

green or crimson bottles — but you drank black coffee by choice, believing that Paris

itself was sufficient alcohol.

— Malcolm Cowley, *Exile's Return: A Literary Odyssey of the 1920s*

AVIGNON

Come, meet me in some dead café—

A puff of cognac or a sip of smoke

Will grant a more prolific light,

Say there is nothing to revoke.

—Lawrence Durrell, (excerpt)

KIKI AT A MONTPARNASSE
RESTAURANT, ca. 1920s
Man Ray

MADELEINE APERITIFS, 1940s
Zelda Fitzgerald

F. SCOTT AND ZELDA
FITZGERALD ON THEIR
HONEYMOON, 1920

W

as it fun? . . . was the Louvre gray and metallic in the sun and
did the trees hang brooding over the cafés?

—Zelda Fitzgerald, in a letter to F. Scott Fitzgerald, Summer 1930

44

CAFÉ LE SELECT, boulevard du
Montparnasse, 1932
Brassaï

B y ten in the evening the whole corner would take on the fullness of its
own life with the terraces crowded and the well-known drunken poets or painters
. . . wandering across the road from café to café.

—Morley Callaghan

That Summer in Paris: Memories of Tangled
Friendships with Hemingway, Fitzgerald, and Some Others

CAFÉ TERRACE AT NIGHT, 1888
Vincent van Gogh

The lights grew bright along the Boulevard St. Michel and the café terraces filled with people. . . . Night settled like a blue blanket over Paris.

—Langston Hughes, *The Big Sea: An Autobiography*

PARIS . . .

Time is of groups. Friends. New ones.

We go to a place together. We are never

left. Big roaring gangs in cafés with

the midst of other roaring gangs.

Godard films it all as if combined,

mirrored into a single side angle.

— Clark Coolidge (excerpt)

CELEBRATION IN MONTPARNASSE AFTER
THE FIRST FUTURIST BALLET, 1929
André Kertész

Left: VIEW OF PEOPLE SEATED
OUTSIDE ON A CAFÉ TERRASSE
Bettman/CORBIS

Right: GALA SOIRÉE AT MAXIM'S, 1949
Brassaï

51

BASTILLE DAY, 1936
Robert Capa

54

It was late and every one had left the café except an old man who sat in the shadow the leaves of the tree made against the electric light. In the day time the street was dusty, but at night the dew settled the dust and the old man liked to sit late because he was deaf and now at night it was quiet and he felt the difference.

—Ernest Hemingway, "A Clean, Well-Lighted Place"

LATE PIQUETTE
James McNeill Whistler

Following page left: AT THE BISTRO, 1932
André Kertész

Following page right: ELIZABETH AND A
FRIEND, Montmartre, 1931
André Kertész

And love: how strangely comfortable love would find itself in this café where everything contrives to provoke looks and glances.

—Louis Aragon, *Paris Peasant*

So there it stood, squeezed between the city and the sea, narrow and humble, with its eight long marble-topped tables standing on heavy iron legs beneath the mirrors that ran the length of the two walls. The leather of the banquettes was split with use and age, and here and there the coils of springs and stuffing had broken through. But still this place seemed extraordinarily luxurious to us.

—Kay Boyle and Robert McAlmon, *Being Geniuses Together*

ELIZABETH AND ME IN A
MONTPARNASSE CAFE, 1931
André Kertész

We sit very close in the café. We walk together very close. We are half sad, half joyous. It is warm. He smells my perfume. I look at his beautiful face. We desire each other.

—Anaïs Nin, *Henry & June: From the Unexpurgated Diary of Anaïs Nin*

LOVERS IN A CAFÉ, ca. 1932
Brassaï

"I am of those who like to stay late at the café," the older waiter said. "With all those who do not want to go to bed. With all those who need a light for the night." "I want to go home and into bed." "We are of two different kinds," the older waiter said. He was now dressed to go home. "It is not only a question of youth and confidence although those things are very beautiful. Each night I am reluctant to close up because there may be some one who needs the café."

—Ernest Hemingway, "A Clean, Well-Lighted Place"

CAFÉ DES 4 VENTS, 1947
René-Jacques

Right: L'HEURE DE L'APERITIF, 1934
Marcel Bovis

ZONE

You stand at the bar of a crapulous café

Drinking coffee at two sous a time in the midst of the

unhappy

You are alone morning is at hand

In the streets the milkmen rattle their cans

—Guillaume Apollinaire,

translated by Samuel Beckett (excerpt)

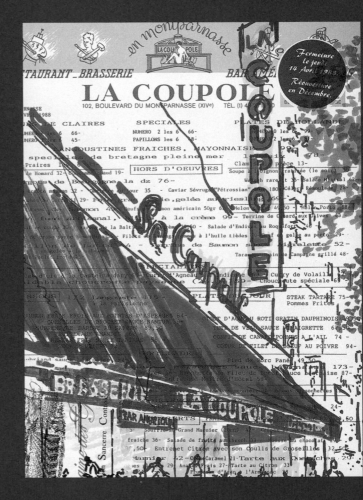

70

F or me, things are looking up. I am elated. I wake up now after five or six hours sleep and am thinking of the next line for my book. At the same time I am thinking in terms of color. I want time too to make a few water colors, at least one or two every day. . . . I have begun to whistle and sing mornings. Oranges first, and then porridge at the Coupole.

—Henry Miller, in a letter to Anaïs Nin, February 27, 1932 (2:00 A.M. Saturday)

LE DOME, Montparnasse, 1932
Brassaï

n a warm summer evening the Dome is at its best, brilliantly lighted, terrace

and interior rooms crowded, all Bohemia there—

—Robert Forrest Wilson, *Paris on Parade*

You arrived at your café at 1 p.m. and stayed until seven. You went out for dinner. You came back at nine and stayed till 2 a.m.

—Jean Moreas

JEUX DE SOCIÉTÉ AU CAFÉ,
rue Lacepede, 1954
Robert Doisneau

A seething madhouse of drunks, semi-drunks, quarter-drunks, and sober maniacs. . . . It was a useless, silly life and I have missed every day since.

—Harold Stearns, *The Street I Know*

The streets were deserted and wet. A fine drizzle enclosed the streetlamps in halos. A few figures were moving close to the houses. On the corner of the Rue Montmartre and the great Boulevards, a café was still open.

—Georges Simenon, *Maigret et la Jeune Morte*

At five o'clock in the morning Guillaume locked the door of the bar behind us. The streets were empty and grey. . . . A *garçon de café* spilled water on the sidewalk before his establishment and swept it into the gutter. At the end of the long, curving street which faced us were the trees of the boulevard and straw chairs piled high before cafés.

— James Baldwin, *Giovanni's Room*

I t ended at last, at daybreak in a bistro near Les Halles, where they had often gone

at dawn for rolls and chocolate or coffee. Outside they could hear the nightly roar and

rumble of the market, the cries of the venders, and smell all sweet smells of earth and

morning, of first light, health, and joy, and day beginning.

—Thomas Wolfe, *Of Time and the River: A Legend of Man's Hunger in His Youth*

STOPPING ALONG THE WAY

Sometimes we used to enter / secret wayside cafés

There might be a step down, / and always there was a table to choose / in the silence
or the murmur of speech.

A shadow was the most ancient of the regulars; / a long, long time she had sat at every
place.

The sun would be there, on good terms with her, / lying upon a forehead, on your
hand, on a glass— / and soon he left, like a god one forgets.

During these halts that seemed to become eternal / experience came to us,

and we always left these secret cafés / subtly changed from what we had been before.

—Guillevic, translated by Denise Levertov

THIS IS A CHAIR—NOTHING MORE, 1931–2
Brassaï

RECIPE FOR HAPPINESS IN KHABAROVSK OR ANYPLACE

One grand boulevard with trees

with one grand café in sun

with small black coffee in very small cups

    one not necessarily beautiful

man or woman who loves you

    one fine day

        —Lawrence Ferlinghetti

JACQUES PREVERT WIT
Robert Doisneau

You end at a café table because everything in Paris ends at a café table.

—Irwin Shaw, *Paris! Paris!*

INDEX OF FEATURED WRITERS

ANDERSON, MARGARET. *The Fiery Fountains: The Autobiography, Continuation and Crisis to 1950.* New York: Horizon Press, 1969. © 1951, 1969 Margaret Anderson.

APOLLINAIRE, GUILLAUME. *Zone.* Translated by Samuel Beckett in *Samuel Beckett: Collected Poems in English and French.* New York: Grove Press, Inc., 1977. © Samuel Beckett Estate, 2002. Reprinted with permission of Calder Publications, Ltd.

ARAGON, LOUIS. *Paris Peasant.* Translated by Simon Watson Taylor. London: Picador, 1987. © 1987 Jonathan Cape, Ltd.

BALDWIN, JAMES. *Giovanni's Room.* New York: Dell Publishing, 1988. © 1956 James Baldwin. Reprinted with permission of Doubleday, a division of Random House, Inc.

BEMELMANS, LUDWIG. *My English Suit in Paris* from *Small Beer.* © 1939 Ludwig Bemelmans. Reprinted with permission of Madeleine Bemelmans and Barbara Bemelmans Marciano.

BOYLE, KAY & ROBERT McALMON. *Being Geniuses Together 1920–1930.* Revised, with supplementary chapters and New Afterword by Kay Boyle. San Francisco: North Point Press, 1984. © 1968 Kay Boyle.

CALLAGHAN, MORLEY. *That Summer in Paris: Memories of Tangled Friendships with Hemingway, Fitzgerald, and Some Others.* New York: Coward-McCann, Inc., 1963. © 1963 Morley Callaghan. Copyright © renewed 1991 Barry Callaghan.

CAMUS, ALBERT. *Notebooks 1935–1942.* Translated by Philip Thody. New York and London: A Harvest/HBJ Book, 1978. © 1963 Hamish Hamilton Ltd., and Alfred A. Knopf, Inc.

——. "Love of Life" from *Lyrical and Critical Essays.* Edited by Philip Thody. Translated by Ellen Conroy Kennedy. New York: Vintage Books, 1979. © 1958 Éditions Gallimard. Permission to reprint granted by Random House, Inc.

CARCO, FRANCIS. *Nostalgie de Paris.* Paris: Editions J. Ferenczi & Fils, 1945. © 1945 J. Ferenczi et Fils.

COOLIDGE, CLARK. *Paris . . .* found in *The Best American Poetry of 1989,* edited by Donald Hall. New York: Collier Books, 1989. © Clark Coolidge. Reprinted with permission by the poet.

COWLEY, MALCOLM. *Exile's Return: A Literary Odyssey of the 1920s.* New York: The Viking Press, 1951. © 1934, 1935, 1941, 1951 Malcolm Cowley. Used with permission of Viking Penguin, a division of Penguin Putnam, Inc.

DAVIS, STUART. *Autobiography.* New York: American Artists' Group, 1945.

DE BEAUVOIR, SIMONE. "Letter to Jean-Paul Sartre [dated 23 January 1941]" in *Letters to Sartre.* Translated and edited by Quintin Hoare. New York: Arcade Publishing, 1992. © 1990 Éditions Gallimard. English translation © 1991 Quintin Hoare. Permission to reprint granted by Little, Brown and Company.

DURRELL, LAWRENCE. *Lawrence Durrell: Collected Poems 1931–1974.* Edited by James A. Brigham. New York: The Viking Press, 1980. © 1980 Lawrence Durrell. Reprinted with permission of Curtis Brown, Ltd., London.

FERLINGHETTI, LAWRENCE. "Recipe for Happiness in Khabarovsk or Anyplace" from *Endless Life.* © 1981 Lawrence Ferlinghetti. Reprinted with permission of New Directions Publishing Corp.

FITZGERALD, F. SCOTT. "Babylon Revisited." Reprinted with permission of Scribner, an imprint of Simon & Schuster Adult Publishing Group, from *The Short Stories of F. Scott Fitzgerald,* edited by Matthew J. Bruccoli. Copyright renewed © 1959 Frances S. Fitzgerald Lanahan.

FITZGERALD, ZELDA. "Letter to F. Scott Fitzgerald" in *Dear Scott, Dearest Zelda: The Love Letters of F. Scott and Zelda Fitzgerald.* Edited by Jackson R. Bryer and Cathy W. Barks. New York: St. Martin's Press, 2002. © 1991 the Trustees under Agreement dated July 3, 1975, created by Frances Scott Fitzgerald Smith.

FLANNER, JANET. *Men & Monuments: Profiles of Picasso, Matisse, Braque, & Malraux.* New York: Da Capo Press, Inc., 1990. © 1979 Natalia Danesi Murray.

GUILLEVIC, EUGENE. "Stopping Along the Way" from *Selected Poems.* Translated by Denise Levertov. © 1968, 1969 Denise Levertov Goodman and Eugene Guillevic. Reprinted with permission of New Directions Publishing Corp.

HEMINGWAY, ERNEST. "A Clean, Well-Lighted Place" from *The Short Stories of Ernest Hemingway.* © 1933 Charles Scribner's Sons. Copyright renewed © 1961 Mary Hemingway.

——. *A Moveable Feast.* New York: A Touchstone Book/Simon & Schuster, 1996. © 1964 Ernest Hemingway Ltd. Copyright renewed © 1992 John H. Hemingway, Patrick Hemingway, and Gregory Hemingway.

HOLMES, OLIVER WENDELL. "Our Hundred Days in Europe" in *The Atlantic Monthly,* Volume LX, September, 1887, No. CCCLIX. © 1897 Oliver Wendell Holmes.

HUGHES, LANGSTON. *The Big Sea: An Autobiography.* New York: Hill and Wang, a division of Farrar, Straus and Giroux, 1994. © 1940 Langston Hughes. Copyright renewed © 1967, 1968 Arna Bontemps and George Houston Bass.

LORD, JAMES. *A Giacometti Portrait.* New York: Farrar Straus Giroux, 1980. © 1980 James Lord. Reprinted with permission of Farrar, Straus and Giroux, LLC.

LUCAS, E. V. *A Wanderer in Paris.* London: Methuen & Co. Ltd., 1909. © 1909, 1924, The Macmillan Company.

MANSFIELD, KATHERINE. "Letter to John Middleton Murry, dated March 19, 1915" in *The Letters of Katherine Mansfield.* Edited by J. Middleton Murry. New York: Alfred Knopf, 1936. © 1929 Alfred A. Knopf, Inc.

MILLER, HENRY. *Henry Miller Letters to Anaïs Nin.* Edited by Gunther Stuhlmann. New York: G. P. Putnam's Sons, 1965. © 1965 Anaïs Nin.

MOREAS, JEAN. Cited in *Elegant Wits and Grand Horizontals: A Sparkling Panorama of* La Belle Epoque: *Its Gilded Society, Irrepressible Wits, and Splendid Courtesans* by Cornelia Otis Skinner. Boston: Houghton Mifflin Company, 1962.

NIN, ANAÏS. *Henry & June: From the Unexpurgated Diary of Anaïs Nin.* By Rupert Pole. San Diego, New York, London: Harcourt Brace Jovanovich Publishers, 1986. © 1986 Rupert Pole as Trustee under the last will and testament of Anaïs Nin.

SARTRE, JEAN-PAUL. *Being and Nothingness: An Essay on Phenomenological Ontology.* Translated by Hazel E. Barnes. New York: Philosophical Library, 1956. © 1956 The Philosophical Library, Inc.

——. "Letter to Simone de Beauvoir [dated summer 1943]" in *Quiet Moments in a War: The Letters of Jean-Paul Sartre to Simone de Beauvoir 1940–1963.* Edited by Simone de Beauvoir. Translated by Lee Fahnestock and Norman MacAfee. New York: Charles Scribner's Sons, 1993.

SHAW, IRWIN AND RONALD SEARLE. *Paris! Paris!* New York and London: Harcourt Brace Jovanovich, 1976. © 1976, 1977 Irwin Shaw.

SIMENON, GEORGES. *Maigret's Memoirs*. Translated by Jean Stewart. New York: Avon Books, 1989. Copyright © 1951 Georges Simenon. English translation Copyright © 1963 Georges Simenon. Published by arrangement with Harcourt Brace Jovanovich, Publishers.

——.*Simenon's Paris*. Text by Georges Simenon. Drawings by Frederick Franck. New York: The Dial Press, 1970.

STEARNS, HAROLD. *The Street I Know*. New York: Lee Furman, Inc., 1935.

WILSON, ROBERT FORREST. *Paris on Parade*. Indianapolis: The Bobbs-Merrill Company Publishers, 1924. Copyright © 1924, 1925 The Bobbs-Merrill Company.

WOLFE, THOMAS. *Of Time and the River: A Legend of Man's Hunger in His Youth*. New York: Charles Scribner's Sons, 1935. © 1935 Charles Scribner's Sons.

INDEX OF FEATURED ARTISTS

ANONYMOUS. *Café de la Paix*. Post card. Author's private collection.

ANONYMOUS. *F. Scott and Zelda Fitzgerald on their Honeymoon*, 1920. *Motor Magazine*.

ANONYMOUS. *Georges Simenon with Josephine Baker, La Coupole, Paris*, 1926. The Simenon Foundation, University of Liege.

ANONYMOUS. *Hemingway (far left) and Friends on a Café Terrace*, 1925. The JFK Library and Museum.

ANONYMOUS. *Le Café de La Paix: rendez-vous du monde entire*. Post card. Author's private collection.

ANONYMOUS. *Montmartre Anuual Waiters' Race*, March 8, 1935. © Fonds France Soir.

ANONYMOUS. *Simone de Beauvoir sitting at her café table in the Flore*. © Papillon/SYGMA.

ANONYMOUS. *View of People Seated Outside on a Café Terrasse*. © Bettmann/CORBIS.

LUDWIG BEMELMANS. *Café des Deux-Magots*. © Madeleine Bemelmans and Barbara Bemelmans Marciano.

——. *Deux-Magots, Madeline's Rescue*. © Madeleine Bemelmans and Barbara Bemelmans Marciano.

JEAN BERAUD. *Femme au Café*, ca. 1890. Oil on canvas, 52 x 46 cm. Union Centrale des Arts décoratifs/Musée des Arts décoratifs, Paris.

EDOUARD BOUBAT. *A La Terrasse des Deux-Magots,* Paris 1955. © Bernard Boubat/RAPHO

MARCEL BOVIS. *L'Heure de L'Apertif,* Paris, 1934. © French Ministry of Culture.

BRASSAÏ. *Café Le Select,* boulevard du Montparnasse, Paris, 1932. © Gilberte Brassaï.

——. *Gala Soiree at Maxim's,* Paris, 1949. Gelatin silver print, 15 x 12 in. (39.4 x 30.5 cm). The Museum of Modern Art, New York. David H. McAlpin Fund. Copy Print © 2002 The Museum of Modern Art, New York. © Gilberte Brassaï.

——. *Jean-Paul Sartre,* Café de Flore, Paris, 1945. © Gilberte Brassaï.

——. *Le Dome,* Montparnasse, Paris, 1932. © Gilberte Brassaï.

——. *Lovers in a Café,* Paris, c. 1932. © Gilberte Brassaï.

——. *Picasso Inside the Café Flore,* 1939. © Gilberte Brassaï.

——. *This is a Chair—Nothing More,* Paris, 1931–2. Gelatin silver print, 11 ¹¹/₁₆ x 9 in. (29.7 x 22.9 cm). The Museum of Modern Art, New York. Gift of Gilberte Brassaï. Digital Image © 2002 The Museum of Modern Art, New York. © Gilberte Brassaï.

ROBERT CAPA. *Bastille Day,* Paris, 1936. © Estate of Robert Capa/Magnum.

——. *Paris, July, 1952.* © Estate of Robert Capa/Magnum.

HENRI CARTIER-BRESSON. *Café,* avenue du Maine, 1932. Copyright © Henri-Cartier Bresson/Magnum Photos.

VAL CLARK. *Café Le Gamin* © Val Clark 2002.

STUART DAVIS. *Blue Café,* 1928. Oil on canvas, 18 ¹/₈ x 21 ⁵/₈ in. Acquired 1930. The Phillips Collection, Washington, D.C.

ROBERT DOISNEAU. *Giacometti in a café,* 1958. © Robert Doisneau/Rapho.

——. *Jacques Prevert with dog,* 1955. © Robert Doisneau/Rapho.

——. *Jeux de Societé au Café,* rue Lacepede, Paris, 1954. © Robert Doisneau/Rapho.

——. *Night view of Les Halles,* 1967. © Robert Doisneau/Rapho.

——. *Simone de Beauvoir in the Café des Deux-Magots,* 1945. © Robert Doisneau/Rapho.

ZELDA FITZGERALD. *Madeleine Aperitifs,* 1940s. Watercolor on paper, 12 ¹/₂ x 17 in. Courtesy of the Scott & Zelda Fitzgerald Museum, Montgomery, Alabama.

RENÉ-JACQUES. *Café des 4 Vents*, 1947. © French Ministry of Culture.

ANDRÉ KERTÉSZ. *Ady's Poem*, © 1928. 231 x 172 mm. © Estate of André Kertész 2002.

——. *At the Bistro*, 1932. © Estate of André Kertész 2002.

——. *Café du Dome, Winter Morning*, Paris, 1928. © Estate of André Kertész 2002.

——. *Celebration in Montparnasse after the First Futurist Ballet*, 1929. © Estate of André Kertész 2002.

——. *The Daisy Bar*, Montmartre, 1930. 241 x 199 mm. © Estate of André Kertész 2002.

——. *Elizabeth and a Friend*, Montmartre, Paris, 1931. © Estate of André Kertész 2002.

——. *Elizabeth and me in a Montparnasse Café*, 1931. © Estate of André Kertész 2002.

SERGIO LARRAIN. *A Saint-Germain-des-Pres*, 1959. © Sergio Larrain/Magnum.

EDOUARD MANET. *Woman Reading*, 1878/9. Oil on canvas, 61.2 x 50.7 cm. Mr. and Mrs. Lewis Larned Coburn Memorial Collection, 1933.435. © The Art Institute of Chicago. All Rights Reserved.

JOHN MINIHAN. *Samuel Beckett at Le Petit Café*, Boulevard St. Jacques, Paris, December 1985. © John Minihan.

LEROY NEIMAN. *La Coupole*. Copyright © LeRoy Neiman, Inc.

PABLO PICASSO. *Bottle, Cup and Newspaper*, Paris, autumn–winter 1912. Pasted paper, charcoal and pencil on paper, 24 3/4 x 18 7/8 in. Museum Folkwang, Essen. © 2002 Estate of Pablo Picasso/Artists Rights Society (ARS), New York.

——. *Le Moulin de la Galette*, Autumn 1900. Oil on canvas, 88.2 x 115.5 cm (34 3/4 x 45 1/2 in.). Solomon R. Guggenheim Museum, New York. Thannhauser Collection, Gift, Justin K. Thannhauser, 1978. 78.2514. 34. Photograph by David Heald. © The Solomon R. Guggenheim Foundation, New York.

CAMILLE PISSARRO. *The Boulevard Montmartre at Night*, 1897. Oil on canvas. 53.3 x 64.8 cm. Bought by the Trustees of the Courtauld Fund, 1925; returned from the Tate Gallery, 1950. © National Gallery, London.

MAN RAY. *Kiki at a Montparnasse Restaurant*, ca. 1920s. Found in *Kiki's Paris: Artists and Lovers 1900–1930* by Billy Kluver and Julie Martin. © Man Ray Trust/ADAGP—Paris/ARS-New York.

SANFORD ROTH. *At the Café Flore in Montparnasse.* Found in *Paris in the Fifties,* Photographs by Sanford Roth. Text by Beulah Roth. Published by Mercury House, Incorporated, 1988, p. 74. © 1988 Beulah Roth.

SEEBERGER BROTHERS. *Café Le Dome,* Paris 1931. Cliché Seeberger frères/Mediathèque de l'Architecture et du Patrimoine/Archives Photographiques. © Centre des monuments nationaux, Paris.

——. *Café Le Dome,* Paris 1931. Cliché Seeberger frères/Mediathèque de l'Architecture et du Patrimoine/Archives Photographiques. © Centre des monuments nationaux, Paris.

D. SPIEGEL. *Café Waiter.* Line drawing. Found in *Paris to the Life: A Sketchbook* by Paul Morand and Doris Spiegel, p. 80. © 1933 Oxford University Press, New York, Inc.

DENNIS STOCK. *Paris, Café de Flore,* 1958. © Dennis Stock/Magnum Photos.

VINCENT VAN GOGH. *Café Terrace at Night,* 1888. © Francis G. Mayer/CORBIS.

JAMES MCNEIL WHISTLER. *Late Piquette.* Lithograph, 7 1/8 x 6 in. Found in *The Whistler Journal* by E. R. & J. Pennell. Philadelphia: J. B. Lippincott Company, 1921, etching W57.